DETECTIVES

by
Hazel Poole

Dog Detectives
Bloodhounds were the first dogs to be used for detective work. Their super-sensitive noses can follow a villain's scent for up to 50 miles.

BRAIN BONUS

Which actor played the first James Bond?

a) Sean Connery
b) David Niven
c) George Lazenby

What does "MI" in MI5 and MI6 stand for?

a) Military Intelligence
b) Major Investigator
c) We can't tell you—it's top secret!

What is the official name for spy activity?

a) snooping
b) sleuthing
c) espionage

(answers on page 32)

PURE GOLD

GoldenEye was the seventeenth Bond film and introduced Pierce Brosnan as 007, making him the fifth actor to play James Bond. The film also starred Judi Dench as M (head of MI6, the British secret service)—the first woman to be Bond's boss.

BOND IS BIG

The twelve original Bond novels, written by Ian Fleming, have sold over 18 million copies worldwide, and 007 has appeared in no less than twenty action-packed films. According to the latest estimates, half of the world's population has seen a Bond film.

Scene from *Goldfinger*

BOND BAD GUYS

Bond has nearly as many enemies as he has fans! They include the likes of Auric Goldfinger, the evil mastermind behind a plan to steal the federal gold reserves—seen here attempting to cut 007 in half with a laser beam. Goldfinger is assisted by his bodyguard and henchman, Oddjob. A martial arts expert, Oddjob is also armed with a hat that, when thrown, can slice the head off a stone statue!

JAMES BOND

The name's Bond—James Bond—but you can call him 007. When it comes to all-action adventure, this super-cool spy guy is licensed to thrill!

REAL INSPIRATION

James Bond was a spy character created in the 1950s by the novelist Ian Fleming. During World War II, Fleming had worked for British naval intelligence and learned lots of spy secrets. He based the character of 007 on two real-life spies—a British hero named Sidney Reilly and a daring double agent called Dusko Popov who obtained top-secret information from the Germans for the FBI.

Pierce Brosnan as James Bond

BOND, THE BIRD-WATCHER

Ian Fleming named his character after the author of *Birds of the West Indies*— a man who preferred bird-watching to saving the world!

GADGETS AND GIZMOS

The equipment used by spies is never what it seems. What at first glance looks like an everyday object turns out on closer inspection to have a secret spy function....

BRAIN BONUS

What name does the CIA give to spy gadgets?
a) sneakers
b) sneakies
c) tweakies

What did spies in World War II hide in cigarette lighters?
a) cigarettes
b) maps
c) compasses

What were small spy cameras called?
a) minicameras
b) pinhole cameras
c) microcameras

(answers on page 32)

GET A "Q"

Before setting off on a mission, James Bond always picks up the latest spy gadget from an inventor code-named "Q." Q's character was based on a real person named Charles Fraser-Smith (1904–1992), who designed top-secret spy equipment for British secret agents during World War II.

SECRET COMPARTMENTS

Coins, pens, and even golf balls have been designed with hidden compartments for concealing secret documents. During World War II, some British agents were armed with hairbrushes! Although they looked ordinary, these brushes had been designed by Charles Fraser-Smith and contained a secret drawer for hiding maps and photographs.

SMALL WONDER

The world's smallest phone "bug" (used for secretly listening to other people's calls) has been nicknamed the "rice grain" by spies. That's because, at just 3/8" long, it's no bigger than a grain of rice!

SECRET WEAPONS

Everyday things can also be adapted to hide weapons. In 1978, Georgi Markov, a Bulgarian writer who criticized his government, was murdered in London by a Bulgarian spy. He was killed by a tiny pellet of poison concealed in the tip of a deadly umbrella that was jabbed into his leg.

Spy camera

IN THE PICTURE

Take a good look at this ring. Smile, please! Despite its ordinary appearance, the ring actually contains a tiny camera. The black spot in the center of the ring is the camera lens. It belonged to a real-life Russian spy and was used for taking secret photographs.

concealing microfilm

BRAIN BONUS

What does the name Mata Hari mean?

a) "dangerous dancer"
b) "eye of the day"
c) "secret agent"

Women served as spies in which war?

a) American Revolution
b) Spanish Civil War
c) World War I

Who is the only American civilian woman to have won the Distinguished Service Cross?

a) Virginia Hall
b) Amy Elizabeth Thorpe
c) Elizabeth Van Lew

(answers on page 32)

"QUEEN OF DISGUISES"

Private eye Annette Kerner could transform her appearance to suit any situation. She once posed as a waitress in a café used by criminals so that she could eavesdrop on them. She even went so far as to disguise herself as a drug addict to capture a gang of opium dealers.

Annette Kerner

SUPER-SPY

Virginia Hall, a one-legged American spy, parachuted into Nazi-occupied France in 1944, clutching her wooden leg under her arm. After organizing the French freedom fighters, she helped them to derail enemy trains and blow up bridges. She radioed military secrets she learned from talkative German soldiers to her spymaster in London. So successful were her efforts that the Nazis began an all-out search for her. She escaped from them (on foot!) over the Pyrenees Mountains into Spain.

LIP SERVICE

The Supercircuits Model PL51XP is a spy video camera small enough to fit in a tube of lipstick. It can beam live pictures up to 450 feet away!

WOMEN SPIES

If you think all spies are men, think again. Many brave women have risked their lives to spy behind enemy lines.

WOMEN AT WAR

One of the most famous female spies of WWI (World War I) was a dancer in France known as Mata Hari. There is no conclusive proof that she was actually a secret agent, but legend has it she pried useful information out of her many French admirers and passed it on to the German secret service. Eventually she was betrayed and captured. During wartime, the penalty if you are caught spying is often death. Mata Hari's case was no exception, and in 1917 she was sent before the firing squad.

Mata Hari

A MODERN MATA HARI

Amy Elizabeth Thorpe (1910–1963) was one of the most successful spies in history. She was an expert at convincing men in key political positions to spill their secrets. This beautiful American spy's dangerous missions took her all over the world. One of her most daring feats of espionage involved stealing top-secret Nazi code-cracking files from the French embassy in Paris.

EYE IN THE SKY

The latest spy planes and satellites give secret agents a great bird's-eye view. But when it comes to espionage, the sky is NOT the limit.

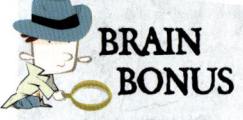

BRAIN BONUS

What is the name of the F-117A Stealth fighter?

a) *Blackbird*
b) *Nightshade*
c) *Nighthawk*

Why must pilots wear spacesuits when flying the Lockheed SR-71?

a) to keep out drafts
b) to disguise themselves
c) to keep their blood from boiling

How long would it take the Lockheed SR-71 to cross the Atlantic Ocean?

a) two hours
b) five hours
c) eight hours

(answers on page 32)

WE HAVE LIFTOFF

Even space is used for spying! Top-secret spy satellites can detect the launch of missiles and provide early warning of an enemy attack. They can also track the movement of soldiers, ships, and tanks—and beam photographs of them back down to Earth.

INVISIBLE PAINT

Most planes show up on radar screens, but the F-117A Stealth fighter plane is coated with a special black paint that absorbs radar signals. It also has radar-jamming equipment on board. As a result, the plane is almost impossible to detect—ideal for secret spying missions!

FAST MOVER

The U.S. Air Force's Lockheed SR-71 is the ultimate spy plane. Not only is it the fastest jet plane in the world, with a top speed of more than 2,100 mph, it can also reach an altitude of almost 99,000 feet—that's more than twice as high as most other planes can go!

Lockheed SR-71

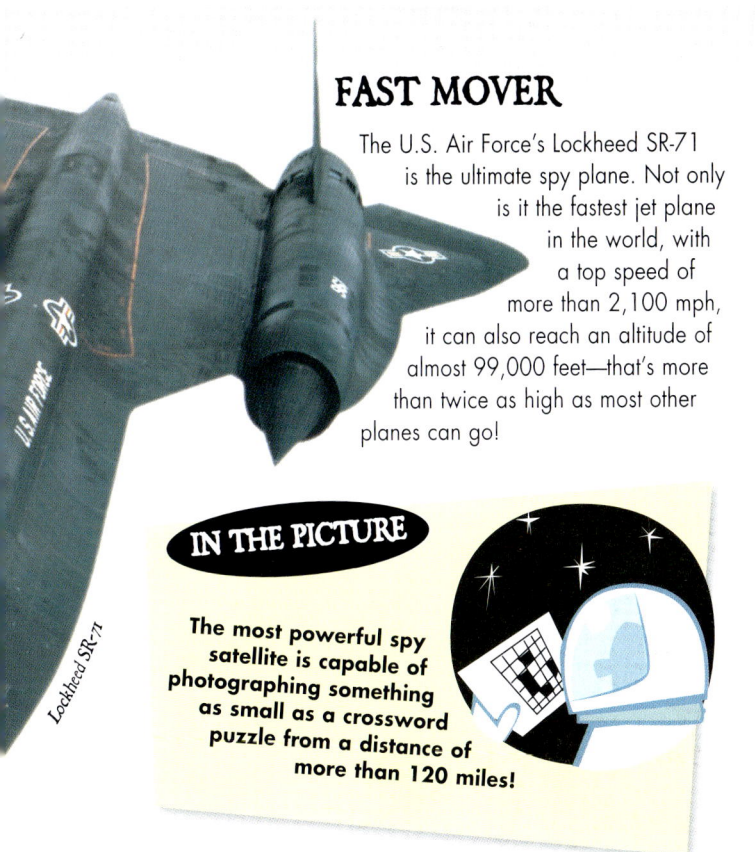

IN THE PICTURE

The most powerful spy satellite is capable of photographing something as small as a crossword puzzle from a distance of more than 120 miles!

IN DEEP WATER

Sleeping Beauty

As well as spies in the sky, there are also spies deep below the waves. This tiny submarine, known as *Sleeping Beauty*, was used by secret agents during World War II. It was so small and quiet that it could creep up close to the enemy without being noticed.

BRAIN BONUS

The most frequently used letter in the English alphabet is...

a) s
b) a
c) e

What is cryptography?

a) the study of crypts
b) the decoding of messages
c) a type of shorthand

Which of the following did Samuel Morse also invent?

a) telegraph
b) telephone
c) radio

(answers on page 32)

International Morse code

A	•–
B	–•••
C	–•–•
D	–••
E	•
F	••–•
G	––•
H	••••
I	••
J	•–––
K	–•–
L	•–••
M	––
N	–•
O	–––
P	•––•
Q	––•–
R	•–•
S	•••
T	–
U	••–
V	•••–
W	•––
X	–••–
Y	–•––
Z	––••
1	•––––
2	••–––
3	•••––
4	••••–
5	•••••
6	–••••
7	––•••
8	–––••
9	––––•
0	–––––

DOTTED LINES

The most famous code of all is called Morse code. It's named after Samuel Morse, the man who developed it in 1838. It was used to send messages by telegraph. Each letter of the alphabet is represented by a series of dots and dashes. How about sending a Morse code message to one of your friends?

SPY SCOUT

Lord Robert Baden-Powell, founder of the International Boy Scouts, served as a spy prior to WWI. His unique skill was creating ornate sketches of butterflies that looked ordinary to the untrained eye yet revealed enemy plans and military fortifications. He used his "butterfly collector" disguise often to escape detection.

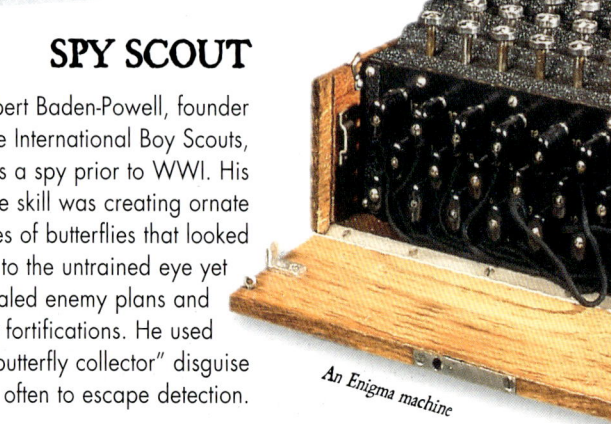

An Enigma machine

CODE-CRACKER

Spies use secret codes when sending messages. That way, even if a message falls into the wrong hands, enemies won't be able to figure out what it means.

WHAT AN ENIGMA

During World War II, German spies sent secret messages using a code called Enigma. To put a message into code, they used a special keyboard like the one in the picture. What the Germans didn't realize was that the Polish secret service had cracked the code a year before the war started!

LISTEN UP

Between 1955 and 1961, British and American spies secretly listened to more than 443,000 phone calls in East Germany—a world record for eavesdropping!

GET CRACKING!

Secret codes are nothing new. Spies have been using them to send messages for hundreds of years. In fact, the first book about codes, explaining how to make them up and crack them, was published back in 1379.

SPY DISGUISE

If you want to be a spy, you must learn how to keep your real identity a secret and observe people without their knowing who you are. To do this, you must become a master of disguise!

FRUIT-FUL IDEAS

Fresh lemon juice makes great invisible ink. When the juice dries, your message will disappear. To make it reappear, simply hold the piece of paper under a hair dryer.

Dark glasses and hat
These help to hide the agent's face so he can't be recognized.

Electronic notepad
To record observations

Binoculars
For observing people at a safe distance

BRAIN BONUS

What was the name of the powerful Soviet secret service?

a) RKO
b) KGB
c) CIA

How many electronic "bugs" does Japan manufacture every year?

a) 24
b) 240
c) 240,000

What type of bird is used to carry messages?

a) pigeon
b) dove

DESPERATE MEASURES

Spies are not the only ones concerned about disguising their appearance. Some criminals will also go to great lengths to avoid being recognized. An outlaw named Ritchie Ramos, for instance, spent $72,000 on plastic surgery while on the run from the police!

LADIES AND GENTLEMEN

One of the most daring and successful disguises was employed by a French spy known as the Chevalier d'Eon. While working as a British double agent, he disguised himself as a woman in order to gain the trust of the empress of Russia. The disguise was so successful that no one knew he was actually a man until he died in 1810!

Mobile phone
To stay in touch with friendly agents

Backpack
For carrying other equipment (such as a camera), plus some different clothes—just in case the spy needs to quickly change his appearance

TOP TIP

A newspaper is one accessory that no good spy should ever be without. It gives you something to pretend to read while you are secretly watching something (or someone) else. What's more, when you hold it up in front of your face, other people can't see what you look like.

BRAIN BONUS

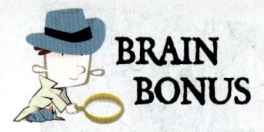

Who was known as the "Ace of Spies"?

a) James Bond
b) Sidney Reilly
c) Guy Burgess

What do you call spies who work for an organization just to learn its secrets?

a) moles
b) bugs
c) mice

What do you call spies who spy on other spies?

a) sleepers
b) watchers
c) rats

(answers on page 32)

DOUBLY DANGEROUS

A double agent is a spy who has secretly changed sides. His old colleagues think he is still working for them when in fact he is passing on all their secrets to the enemy. In 1996, CIA officer Harold Nicholson was arrested at an airport by the FBI, who suspected that he was a dangerous double agent. They were right! Nicholson was on his way to hand over rolls of film containing top-secret U.S. information to the Russians.

ZZZZZZ

A sleeper is a spy whose mission is to fit into mainstream society until his skills are needed for a special task, such as sabotage.

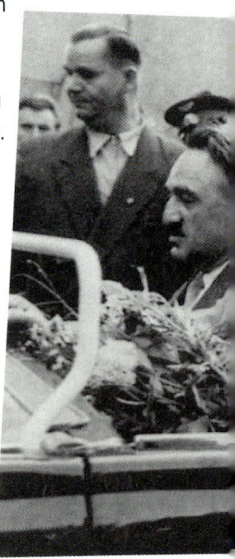

DEAD DROP

A secret dead drop

A dead drop is a place where spies can secretly leave messages for each other or collect them. In the 1980s, the KGB (the former Soviet Union's secret spy organization) used a marble column in a London church as a dead drop. A small blue mark on a lamppost outside the church showed agents that a message was waiting. A white mark on a bench nearby meant the message had been picked up.

SPY LINGO

If you really want to understand the cloak-and-dagger world of espionage, you'll have to learn some of the slang spies use.

SPYMASTER

A senior spy who is in charge of other secret agents is often known as a spymaster. This photograph shows a spymaster named Markus Wolf—known as "the man without a face" because for many years no one knew what he looked like. Wolf worked for the East German secret police and was responsible for organizing spying operations in foreign countries.

MICRODOT

During World War II, German spies sent secret documents to each other by shrinking them to 1/400th of their original size. Known as microdots, they were small enough to be hidden on the edge of a postcard!

SPIES AGAINST CRIMES

Not all agents spy on foreign countries. Some are busy closer to home fighting crime—and spying on other spies!

FBI AND CIA

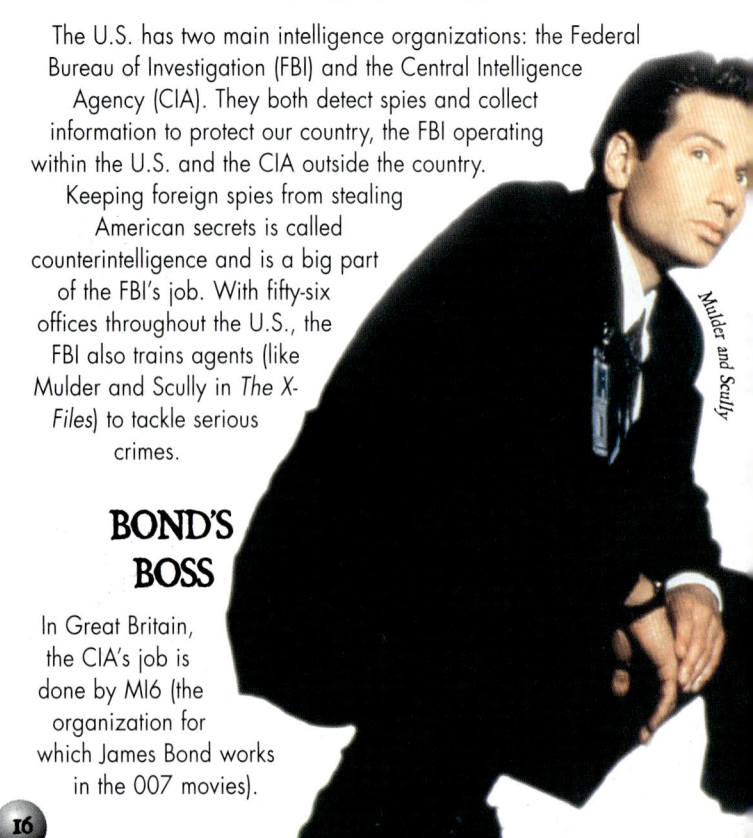

The U.S. has two main intelligence organizations: the Federal Bureau of Investigation (FBI) and the Central Intelligence Agency (CIA). They both detect spies and collect information to protect our country, the FBI operating within the U.S. and the CIA outside the country.

Keeping foreign spies from stealing American secrets is called counterintelligence and is a big part of the FBI's job. With fifty-six offices throughout the U.S., the FBI also trains agents (like Mulder and Scully in *The X-Files*) to tackle serious crimes.

Mulder and Scully

BOND'S BOSS

In Great Britain, the CIA's job is done by MI6 (the organization for which James Bond works in the 007 movies).

THE SPY NEXT DOOR

Before the end of the Cold War in 1991, East Germany had more spies than any other country. Most were ordinary people who were encouraged to spy on their neighbors. By 1985, one in every fifty people living there was a spy!

TOP SECRET

MI5, the British counterpart to the FBI, was formed in 1909—although its activities were so secret that the government didn't officially admit it existed until 1989! Agents working for MI5 have the power to investigate anyone who might threaten Britain's national security.

SPY FILES

Security organizations such as MI5 and the CIA hold intelligence files on known criminals and foreign spies. These files contain details about where they live, where they like to go, the names they use, and all kinds of other useful information!

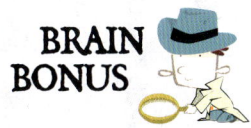

BRAIN BONUS

In *The X-Files*, what does Agent Mulder believe in that Agent Scully is unsure of?

a) leprechauns
b) Santa Claus
c) aliens

Who headed the FBI from 1924 to 1972?

a) J. Edgar Hoover
b) Richard Nixon
c) Harry Palmer

_____ American companies spy on their employees using video cameras.

a) 1 in every 500
b) 1 in every 100
c) 1 in every 10

(answers on page 32)

Spy files

AN EYE ON THE WORLD

BRAIN BONUS

Which movie spy is called the "International Man of Mystery"?
a) Inspector Gadget
b) Inspector Clouseau
c) Austin Powers

What's a Top 10 fugitive?
a) an award-winning spy
b) a criminal wanted by the FBI
c) a smuggler who gambles

Which endangered animals are often smuggled into the U.S. to be sold illegally to the pet trade?
a) parrots
b) snakes
c) turtles

(answers on page 32)

Crime is an international problem. To tackle the biggest criminal operations, police forces in different countries must work together. And that's where Interpol comes in.

INTERNATIONAL RESCUE

The International Criminal Police Organization (known as Interpol for short) was formed in 1923. It is made up of police forces from 177 countries. Interpol enables different police organizations to share information, such as fingerprint records. It's a major weapon in the fight against organized crime around the world.

Marijuana

GET OUT OF BED OR DIE! The most severe lawmaker was an ancient Greek called Draco. In 621 B.C., he made almost every crime punishable by execution—even laziness!

MONEY, MONEY, MONEY!

Drug smuggling is big business. In 1989, following a long undercover surveillance operation, police in the U.S. pounced on a gang of international smugglers and seized drugs worth around $8.6 billion.

THE MAFIA MOB

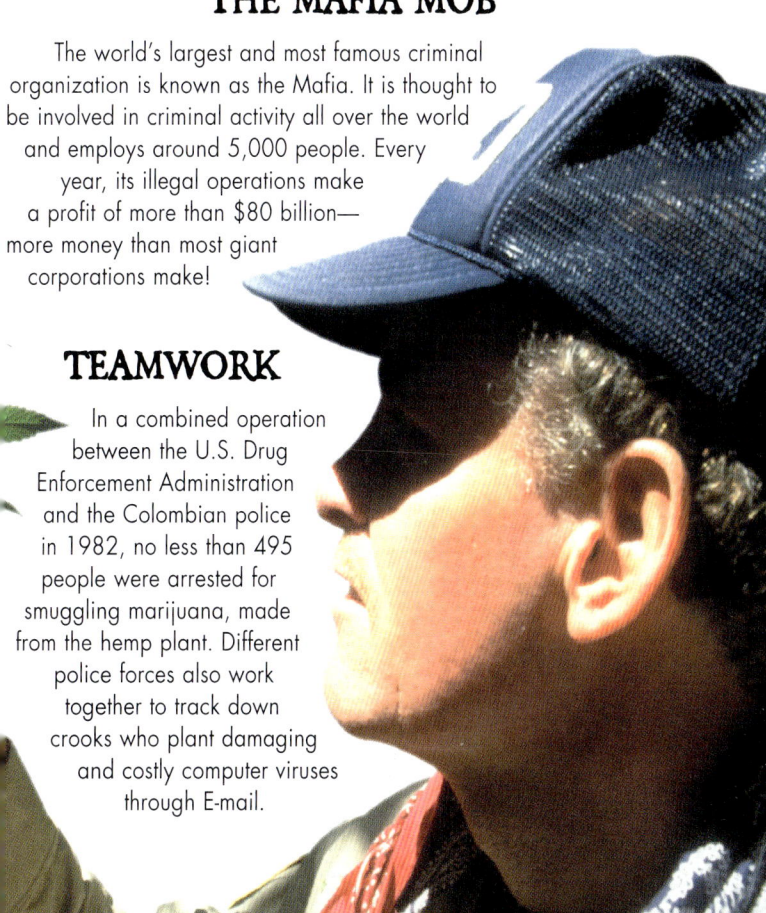

The world's largest and most famous criminal organization is known as the Mafia. It is thought to be involved in criminal activity all over the world and employs around 5,000 people. Every year, its illegal operations make a profit of more than $80 billion—more money than most giant corporations make!

TEAMWORK

In a combined operation between the U.S. Drug Enforcement Administration and the Colombian police in 1982, no less than 495 people were arrested for smuggling marijuana, made from the hemp plant. Different police forces also work together to track down crooks who plant damaging and costly computer viruses through E-mail.

CRIME BOSS CAPONE

Al Capone

In 1919, alcohol was outlawed in the U.S. This provided gangsters with the perfect opportunity to make money by bootlegging (selling alcohol illegally). Al Capone ran the bootlegging operation in the city of Chicago and defended his territory fiercely. It is thought that he was involved in more than 1,000 murders.

BRAIN BONUS

What does the Secret Service do today?
a) sells U.S. secrets
b) chases train robbers
c) protects the president and his family

By what name was Al Capone also known?
a) Scarface
b) The Godfather
c) The Boss

What is a "moll"?
a) a place where spies shop
b) a gangster's girlfriend
c) Al Capone's favorite candy

(answers on page 32)

WHAT A RACKET

The first detectives to patrol the streets of London carried rattles in their coattails. When they were chasing a criminal, they would wave the rattle to raise the alarm.

THE UNTOUCHABLES

In the early part of this century, a great detective hero appeared in America. His name was Eliot Ness, and he was responsible for finally putting Al Capone behind bars. Ness and his team became known as "The Untouchables" because they refused to be bribed or bullied by criminals.

EARLY DETECTIVES

The earliest crime-busters really had their work cut out for them—vicious gangsters made sure there was trouble.

A sheriff dressed in Wild West style

EYE SAY!

The oldest private-detective agency in the world was set up by Allan Pinkerton back in 1850. The Pinkerton detective agency is still going strong today. Its trademark is an open eye—which gave rise to the term "private eye," meaning a private detective.

STAR SHERIFF

Pinkerton began his career as a county sheriff and brought several notorious Wild West outlaws to justice—including a band of train robbers called the Reno brothers. He also uncovered an early assassination plot against Abraham Lincoln just before Lincoln became president. Lincoln made Pinkerton his spymaster and head of the brand-new Secret Service, which at that time was in charge of tracking down gangs of counterfeiters (criminals who make fake money).

BRAIN BONUS

Which of these fictional detectives has a photographic memory?
a) Encyclopedia Brown
b) Cam Jansen
c) Nancy Drew

What gets Harriet in trouble with her friends in the book *Harriet the Spy*?
a) her secret notebooks
b) her stinky tennis shoes
c) her late-night phone calls

Who is known for solving science mysteries?
a) Mr. Pin
b) Bunnicula
c) Einstein Anderson

(answers on page 32)

BACK FROM THE DEAD

With his trademark pipe and deerstalker hat, Sherlock Holmes quickly became very popular. Then, in 1894, Sir Arthur Conan Doyle wrote a story in which Holmes was killed. The detective's fans were furious. In fact, the public outcry was so huge that Doyle had to write another story to bring Holmes back to life!

FACT NOT FICTION

Sir Arthur Conan Doyle was a real-life amateur detective and actually helped to solve several crimes in England.

CHRISTIE'S CHARACTERS

The author Agatha Christie came up with not one but two great detective characters—a white-haired old lady named Miss Marple and a fussy Belgian with a curly mustache named Hercule Poirot. All of Christie's murder mysteries are famous for the clever twists in their plots—the murderer is always the person you least expect it to be!

David Suchet as Hercule Poirot

FICTIONAL DETECTIVES

The first detective story ever written, "The Murders in the Rue Morgue" (1841), was by an author named Edgar Allan Poe and featured a crime-busting super-sleuth named C. Auguste Dupin.

PARTNERS IN CRIME

The most famous detective character of all is Sherlock Holmes. More than 200 movies have been made of his adventures—making him the most portrayed character of all time. Holmes and his trusty companion, Dr. Watson, were created by the British novelist Sir Arthur Conan Doyle, who wrote no less than 68 detective stories.

EAGLE EYES

Doyle based the character of Holmes partly on a real person named Joseph Bell. Bell was a doctor who became famous for figuring out what was wrong with his patients by observing them very closely. It was exactly this kind of eagle-eyed observation that enabled Holmes to solve some of his most baffling cases.

Basil Rathbone as Sherlock Holmes

DOG DETECTIVES

Our four-legged friends have been helping the police catch criminals since the 1800s. With such smart police dogs around, crooks had better watch out—especially cat burglars!

ON THE SCENT

The first dogs used for detective work were bloodhounds. With their super-sensitive noses, they can follow the scent of an outlaw on the run—even if there is no trace of footprints. In fact, once they get a whiff of a villain, bloodhounds have been known to follow their noses for up to 50 miles.

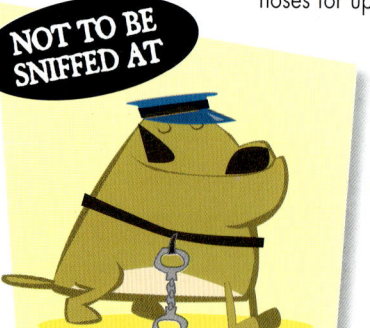

NOT TO BE SNIFFED AT

DRESSED FOR THE JOB

Police dogs in some forces even have their own special uniforms! These include a bulletproof vest, boots to protect the dog's paws, and a special harness containing a video camera that can be attached to the dog's head.

Dogs' noses are thousands of times more sensitive than human noses.

TOUGH TRAINING

Most police dogs these days are German shepherds or Labradors. Before they join the force, they must pass a tough 14-week basic training course. Only pups that make the grade go on to learn advanced skills, like how to sniff out drugs and explosives or disarm someone with a gun.

A German shepherd in training

A police bloodhound

TOP DOG

One of the most famous police dogs of all time was named Rex III. He worked for a division of the British police known as the Flying Squad and was the first police dog to be used to detect illegal drugs. During his distinguished career, he helped arrest more than 130 suspects and was awarded several medals.

BRAIN BONUS

What are German shepherds also called?

a) Alsatians
b) Labradors
c) Rottweilers

What are dog detectives trained to do?

a) find bodies under water
b) jump through open windows
c) climb ladders

What cartoon dog detective has a partner named Shaggy?

a) Lassie
b) Scrappy
c) Scooby-Doo

(answers on page 32)

POINTING THE FINGER

The tiny grooves on the tips of your fingers leave fingerprints on everything you touch. Everyone's fingerprints are different, which means they can be used to identify who you are. Detectives started looking for fingerprints in the 1800s. The FBI currently has 230 million sets in its collection—the largest in the world.

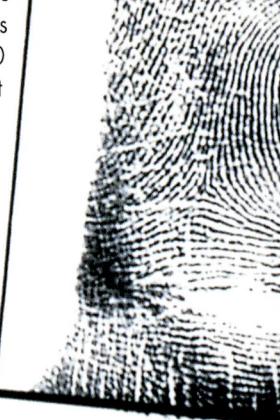

A loop fingerprint

9. L. RING

GOTCHA!

Detectives used to dust only for fingerprints left on slick surfaces like glass or metal by brushing on a very fine powder that would stick to the prints. Then they discovered that invisible prints were also left on porous surfaces like paper and skin. These could only be seen when the surface was treated with chemicals or exposed to lasers. Now detectives can find fingerprints left on very old documents!

BRAIN BONUS

How many blood types are there?
a) 3
b) 4
c) 5

When dusting a dark surface for fingerprints, what should you use?
a) black powder
b) white powder
c) red powder

Loop, arch, and _____: which of the three main fingerprint types is missing?
a) wheel
b) whirl
c) whorl

(answers on page 32)

GOT IT LICKED

It's not just your fingerprints or DNA that are unique. Like your fingers, your tongue is covered in a pattern of grooves, and no two people have exactly the same tongue print, either!

CRIME SCENE

When they get to the scene of a crime, detectives start looking for clues.

MAGIC MOLECULE

Every cell in your body contains deoxyribonucleic acid, known as DNA for short. DNA is complicated stuff—it's what makes us who we are. No two people have exactly the same DNA.

PERSONAL BAR CODES

By taking a sample of body tissue (such as blood, hair, or skin), crime scientists can create a "DNA fingerprint." It looks a little bit like the bar codes printed on merchandise. They can then compare this with the DNA of their suspects. A match can often be used to prove whether someone is innocent or guilty.

A model of DNA cells

CLUE CATCHER

But what if the criminal has scrubbed away all the clues? This is almost impossible, thanks to chemicals such as Luminol. Police scientists spray it and then shine ultraviolet light on it. Invisible bloodstains can be seen on the surface up to two years after they've been washed off!

CLOSING THE TRAP

Once detectives have identified their suspect, they set out to gather enough evidence to prove that this person is guilty. Here's how!

BIG DEAL

An electron microscope is used to examine tiny fibers found at a crime scene. It can magnify objects more than 150,000 times. If you were magnified this much, you would be 17 times the height of Mount Everest!

WITNESS STATEMENTS

Detectives spend time talking to witnesses and checking out the suspects' alibis (what they claim they were doing or whom they were with when the crime happened). Each witness is carefully interviewed, and their words are recorded as a statement for use in court during a trial.

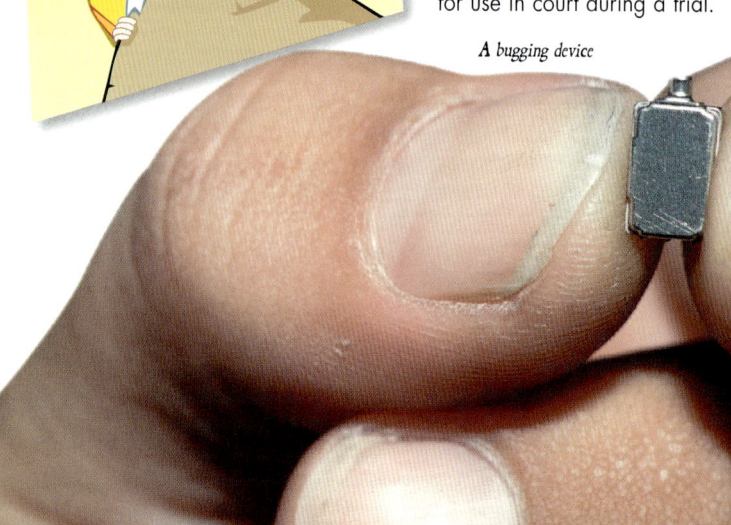

A bugging device

A polygraph

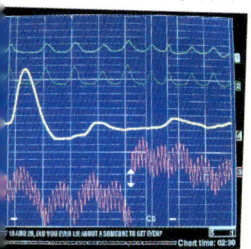

THE WHOLE TRUTH?

Lie detectors (or polygraphs) measure tiny changes in a suspect's blood pressure, heartbeat, and breathing as he or she answers questions. This information can be used as a guide to tell whether or not the person is telling the truth. The results appear on a graph like the one above. The polygraph was first used in 1924, but results are rarely accepted as evidence during court trials now because they are not reliable enough.

ON THE RIGHT TRACK

Tracking devices, known as bumper beepers, can be secretly attached to cars so that police can follow their every move from a safe distance. The beeper is actually a tiny radio transmitter that sends out an electronic signal wherever it goes.

STOP BUGGING ME!

Hidden microphones, called bugs, are sometimes installed in a suspect's home so detectives can listen to what this person says. Some microphones, like the one in the picture, are small enough to be hidden behind a poster or under a table without anyone noticing.

BRAIN BONUS

What is another name for a postmortem?

a) autoplasty
b) biopsy
c) autopsy

Which case made kidnapping a federal crime?

a) The Missing Mom Case
b) The Beanie Baby Caper
c) The Lindbergh Baby Case

Which famous couple was executed in 1953 for spying?

a) Julius and Ethel Rosenberg
b) Aldrich and Rosario Ames
c) Barney and Betty Rubble

(answers on page 32)

BRAIN BONUS

What is a scrambler?
a) a type of lie detector
b) a device for keeping calls private
c) a machine used for writing secret code

What is the illegal copying of videos or CDs called?
a) piracy
b) duplicity
c) mastering

Which industry is often threatened by the prying eyes of industrial spies?
a) fashion
b) automobile
c) entertainment

(answers on page 32)

ARMCHAIR DETECTIVES

In many countries, television programs enable viewers at home to help detectives solve real-life crimes. These shows feature crime reenactments (where actors play the parts of criminals), stolen or missing property, and pictures of people the police would like to interview. Viewers can then call in with any useful information they have.

NEW CRIME BOOM

One of the biggest crime problems today is so-called white-collar crime. Most of these crimes are committed by employees to give the companies they work for an unfair advantage over rival firms—for example, by illegal price-fixing, fraud, or industrial espionage. It is estimated that in the United States alone, white-collar crime is worth around $200 billion every year—ten times the cost of all the burglaries, thefts, and robberies put together!

Modern private eyes

PRIVATE EYES, PRIVATE SPIES

Private investigators play a major part in modern law enforcement. Often they are hired to track down people who have gone into hiding to avoid giving evidence in court. Their work also includes searching for missing people and helping companies to detect dishonest employees.

DETECTIVES TODAY

Today's detectives must learn new skills to tackle new types of crime. Meanwhile, ordinary people can play their part in bringing outlaws to justice—by watching television.

ROBO-COPS

The fastest crime-busters today are computers—they match fingerprints found at a crime scene at a rate of 60,000 per second!

modern detective on a case

WATCH OUT!

Private eyes and undercover agents are secretly at work all around us—in shopping malls, in airports, on the Internet, and in lots of other unexpected places. You never know who might be watching you!

BRAIN BONUS ANSWERS

p. 2 a) Sean Connery. a) Military Intelligence. c) espionage.

p. 4 b) sneakies. c) compasses. b) pinhole cameras.

p. 6 b) "eye of the day," i.e., the sun.
a) b) c) Female spies have served in all three of these wars, as well as many others.
c) Virginia Hall.

p. 8 c) *Nighthawk*. c) to keep their blood from boiling under the extreme pressure and heat.
a) two hours.

p. 10 c) the letter e. b) the decoding of messages.
a) Morse invented the telegraph in 1838.

p. 12 b) KGB, in operation (under various names) from 1917 to 1991.
c) 240,000. a) pigeon.

p. 14 b) Sidney Reilly, Britain's most important secret agent before WWI. He spoke seven languages.
a) moles. b) watchers.

p. 17 c) aliens. a) J. Edgar Hoover, who grew so powerful that he was in a position to blackmail politicians—including the president. c) 1 in every 10.

p. 18 c) Austin Powers. b) a criminal wanted by the FBI. a) b) c) parrots, snakes, and turtles. Many endangered animals die during their illegal journey because they are not handled properly by the smugglers.

p. 20 c) protects the president and his family. a) Scarface. b) a gangster's girlfriend.

p. 22 b) Cam Jansen. a) her secret notebooks. c) Einstein Anderson.

p. 25 a) Alsatians. a) b) c) All three. Dog detectives are amazing! c) Scooby-Doo.

p. 26 b) There are four blood types (A, B, AB, and O). b) white powder. c) whorl.

p. 29 c) autopsy. c) The Lindbergh Baby Case. a) Julius and Ethel Rosenberg. They were accused of delivering U.S. weapons secrets to the Soviet Union, though they never confessed to the crime.

p. 30 b) a device for keeping calls private. a) piracy. a) b) c) fashion, automobile, entertainment.